ENLIGHTENMENT
IN DEPRESSION

ENLIGHTENMENT IN DEPRESSION

Succeed Under Pressure as Testing Times Pass By to Reveal the Merit of Endurance

Sathish Kumar Mahalingam

PARTRIDGE

A Penguin Random House Company

ISBN: Hardcover   978-1-4828-3447-5
             Softcover   978-1-4828-3446-8
             eBook   978-1-4828-3445-1

To order additional copies of this book, contact
Partridge India
000 800 10062 62
orders.india@partridgepublishing.com

www.partridgepublishing.com/india

Contents

For my family, who believed from the beginning, and especially my wife, Radha, who patiently saw me through to the end.

Preface

I had a humble beginning when I started my life. Today I am proud to spread the message of endurance. I am a success story now, and I am a living example of head held high. There were times in my early adulthood when I had lost hope, but somehow I survived, and time and life taught me the secret of not losing hope and fighting back every time things make you fall.

I will reveal the secret of winning when you are put down. Say, 'I will succeed, and let my success story be known to all who belittled me.' Strive to endure, and strive to succeed. When you encounter challenges, never give up, and you will ultimately win as I have. Every effort you put to uplift yourself will surely make you stronger and accelerate your pace toward this effort. Say, 'I have sowed the seeds now, and no matter what, I will reap the harvest.' This is an autobiography of my early life, but the wealth of the message is too important to ignore.

Love and Wisdom

With a sudden vibration within Sathish's head, he awoke in the middle of the night. Sathish could sense the whir of the chip implanted into his brain. He did not know how it was possible for them to do so without his knowledge. All that he knew was that he had unusual sleeping and waking times. He was an engineer and a biology student till his twelfth grade, and it was not the first time that he sensed this vibration. Only after a repetition of such incidents did he come to this conclusion.

On the first few weeks of his arrival in the US from India, he was okay, but as days went by, the problem hidden inside him slowly began to emerge. Since his twelfth grade onward, he had suffered from depression. Were those vibrations hallucinations because of depression, or were they real? He had no way to prove to anyone, nor did he want to. Despite being in depression in India there was no such feeling in him then. This was what had added credibility to his findings.

His education was from a school run by missionaries who treated children in a very harsh way with corporal punishments, like caning and frequent threats. He had studied in this school since he was in the lower kindergarten. These missionaries were converts. They had lost faith in their faith and endorsed a different faith, thinking that they would be faithful to the newfound faith. They used to frequently talk about discipline. To them, discipline was what they used to make the students obey, but they themselves flouted the directions of the state government.

They used to say that their institution was a private minority institution, not realizing that India was not a private minority government and that every person was a private minority individual. The maximum number of staff and students belonged to the majority of the community. He underwent electroconvulsive therapy two times after consulting a psychiatrist in India. This repression made him a rebel against such confinement of children and youth after he left school.

He faced ragging in college, and he completed college only after an extra year. Ragging was allowed by the college management as a trick so that students would be divided and their unity spoiled. This they hoped would prevent the students from turning against the college management, which did not provide even the basic amenities, like the choice of the elective which they preferred.

Prior to joining a software company in Chennai, India, he worked in a call center. During this period, he engaged in sex by indulging in wild fantasies, masturbating at least thrice a day when no one was there at the house where he stayed. He longed for a sex partner and a private confidant. But he never sought a prostitute.

He was an avid listener of Osho's audiobooks. Sathish used to start his day in the middle of the night. It was day in the USA when it was night in India. His team consisted of a small group of ten persons working for a big online-shopping giant. It was there that he saw her. Madhu was her name. Charming and always cheerful was her face, and slim was her structure. She wasn't shy, and she gracefully chatted with friends. Sathish was reserved; he only opened his mouth to utter a few words when someone spoke to him.

Being enchanted by this beauty and having researched her qualities which he lacked, he took the bold decision of going to her and asking her, 'I like you. *Yes* solicited.' She said she was engaged, but he thought that this was her pretext to avoid such proposals. Sathish waited for two days, still not receiving any reply. He then walked up to her cabin and requested her to write her e-mail address on a paper, which she consented to. He then wrote a letter to her.

This was his letter of clarification to someone of the opposite sex who was confusing him. He needed an explanation. And I got it, but he was only able to take it factually. In the great depths of his mind, even to this day, he is not able to take the response he got. Whatever it was, it served the cause of furthering his creativity and appreciation of beauty the way it should be.

Clarification required.
This message is personal and not from an anonymous person.

From Sathish. (You would have seen me in the office. I have spoken to you in six instances.)

Do you remember the first request I made to you?

Explicit request: 'I like you. *Yes* solicited.' I hope you understand what 'I like you' in Tamil means when the request comes from a person of my age to a person of your age.

You said you were engaged. But you have been giving me conflicting signs from which I make assumptions of what they could mean implicitly.

I understand that you have no obligations toward me. At this juncture, I still request for you to give me a firm affirmation or negation (yes or no). This would relieve me of my confusion and help me fully stop thinking about a person who could belong to someone else.

Thank you for your patience. I apologize for the disturbance that has been caused.

Note: This message is deliberately composed to be less in passion and feelings. In case of an affirmation, all efforts will be made to accommodate emotions.

She gave a reply.

I am writing this just to clarify things.

I have no so-called feelings for you.

You are just another person whom I meet at my workplace.

Do keep this in mind.

It's true that I am engaged. But you have nothing to do with it.

I do not understand what you mean by 'conflicting signs'.

It was my mistake that I responded to you politely whenever you spoke to me.

I just respected you for your age.

I will not encourage any kind of contact or response from you anymore.

If you try to have further contacts with me, my friends here might have to get involved in this issue.

From
Madhu

He could have taken this forward, but his skepticism made him go back because this message from her never said that she rejected Sathish. He resigned from his job and joined a software company in Chennai. Sathish's performance was well, and he was asked whether he wanted to go to the USA to the onshore development center. When offered a chance to become employed in a US company, he at first felt uninterested given his dependence on medication for depression.

Sathish's father came to know about this offer. It was his father who was interested in sending him to the USA so that he could achieve more in life. He accepted his father's choice and agreed to go to the USA. He got his H1B visa and happily bought new clothes and other items that he felt may be needed in the USA.

A date was fixed for his first flight. A few of his friends—Arun, Sanjay, and Ashok (who were working with him)—also accompanied him. Ashok was his closest friend in this set. This was because while in Chennai, they had shared the same room in a mansion. Arun was a bit of an intellectual fluent in English and was a chat friend when Sathish got drunk. Arun though did not have any bad habits. After he landed in Atlanta, he was received by an official in his US office.

While being driven to his apartment in Duluth, which the US office had arranged for him and his friends, he experienced the grandeur and splendor of the USA in its multilane roads with big trucks and speeding cars. They reached the apartment and were given tips about how to overcome the jet lag. On the next morning at 9 a.m., they were taken to the office in Suwanee near Duluth.

He felt the door of opportunity open before his eyes when he was given a small orientation about life and work in the USA.

A few weeks went by, and he got his Social Security number. He bought a mobile phone out of the first month's pay.

His marketing manager, Mr. David, requested Sathish to prepare a *résumé* and get ready for the interview process by his company's clients. Sathish was an enterprise resource planning consultant. He knew a programming language called ABAP (advanced business application programming) developed by a German company called SAP. He knew the functional aspects of sales and distribution and material management.

Meanwhile, he got a driver's license after three failed attempts. He passed the online test, but the road test was successful only after three attempts. While most of his friends accomplished this in the first attempt, he did not do it. Did it have something to do with the authorities knowing his psychiatric condition? A small doubt started to linger in his mind.

At the office, he was busy with the projects, but all this was just for two months. One day his friends asked him whether he could join them on a trip to Savannah. This proposal was made two days ahead of the trip which was to start on a Friday night and end on Sunday night. Everyone was friendly, but on that Friday night when the trip was about to begin, his friends started to make indirect references to him and started insulting him in an indirect way.

What could the reason be? he thought. *Was it that they had come to know the letter he had sent to the American Consulate in Chennai, India?*

While in Chennai, Sathish had written to the American Consulate, complaining about the large sum of money his company demanded to sponsor an H1B visa. This complaint had made an impact since from then on, the employees of that company had to go to the American Consulate in Delhi to get their visas approved. So now he feared that his company was planning its revenge.

Sathish told his friends that he—though an old man in the mind—was only 29 in age and was reasonably young. He told them that if they continued their tirade, he did not want to join them. One of his close friends, Suresh, told him that he could relax. So the two-day journey started, which he enjoyed a lot. His face had appeared retarded since the past two weeks, and his speech was confusing between what others understood implicitly and explicitly.

Now he was in the US as his father had wished, but he was engulfed in depression; his medication did not work as desired. Its side effects made his mood dull and made his fingers shaky.

He sought loneliness and moved away from his friends. He did not work the full eight hours in his office, and hallucinations made him hypersensitive. He became excited and irritable at even the very small sound he could hear. He craved for a sexual partner, but since his first love story had failed him, he did not want to make a new proposal. He thought that pursuing his first love with Madhu could in a way work out.

He knew he had become a maniac, and all things that surrounded him made him suspicious. But he decided to be worthwhile even in this condition. So he decided to contribute good while some countries were sponsoring mercenaries for terrorism.

So on each night when he woke up, he composed the following lines at the rate of one topic per day. After completion of the written topic, he uploaded it to his e-mail inbox, hoping that people spying on him would easily have access to his work.

Let us now see what he wrote, for which he himself has given an explanation.

These lines were written out of desperation and craving for sex. There is a sort of justification for the release of sexual energy that gets accumulated and spoils the day-to-day activities. This is a personification of the male sex organ. This part of prose shows how the feeling of sex is also an integral part of a healthy being.

Creative Writing

You see that this fellow called the p***s wants me to cater to his needs. I exercise suppression and control him. If I keep ill-treating him, he may seek liberation and become a rebel. He may spoil my integrity and unity. I want to treat him reasonably. You see, he is also a valuable part of my wholeness. What am I going to achieve by treating him like this? This ill treatment makes even the very basic processes of my life difficult.

United I stand; divided I fall.

Unity in diversity.

These lines reflect how he sees God. He has in these lines depicted God as all-caring and all-loving. God does not look into differences in accommodating his children in the magnificence of his creation.

I see the Almighty, the Omnipotent, and the All-Pervading in a secular, unbiased form. He or she is not the one who demands that I clip my teeth, grow fingernails, cut my toenails, or sport a mustache. He or she is also the one who cares for his or her children with all such varied beliefs. He or she gives the freedom to represent him or her in whatever form that can be perceived.

My Religion

These lines were written in order for him to have a justification for pursuing love which could de facto be beyond his means. These lines show how one can derive the inspiration and means to pursue his or her desire.

Inspiration

I belong to the nation of the Mahatma.

Was it not a great expectation at his time that he sought freedom for his country?

And what was the means that he employed? Was it ever expected?

Whatever people may want me to expect, I don't fear to expect the unexpected.

Thank you, my friend, for the constructive provocation.

These lines were written to show that masturbation is faking. If faking itself can give this much benefit, imagine how the real thing could contribute to one's well-being.

Benefits of Fake Sex or Masturbation

1. Relieves one of any physical pain
2. Gives a good sleep
3. Helps smoothen hurtful memories
4. Improves imagination
5. Helps concentration
6. Burns calories
7. Releases accumulated anger
8. Improves blood circulation
9. Gives fake pleasure
10. Relaxes the mind and body.

Drawback

1. Too much of it can cause memory loss.
2. It does not much matter as long as you know how to handle it.

Benefits of true sex.

Big? Mark

Inspiration: even Vatsyayana was born in my country.

There are many art forms. The art form that he is mentioning here is the art by which all other arts can be appreciated. This art form is the basis for all higher levels of human development. He has also cited some examples.

Beauty

Of all the great arts, the greatest is the art of appreciation of beauty. If not for this art, there would not have been civilization nor invention, curiosity nor discovery, generosity nor prudence, courage nor sacrifice, wisdom nor intellect, love nor brotherhood, power nor modesty, all the goodness in this world that we see now.

Random examples: nature, Mahatma Gandhi, Swami Vivekananda, Egyptian civilization, Indus Valley civilization, airplane, fire, God, child, Columbus, Mother Teresa, Winston Churchill, Rani Lakshmibai, Chanakya, Einstein, and Shah Jahan.

This is a small poem which he wrote in remembrance of his dream girl or lover. These lines show how he would like her to be a source of inspiration in his life.

Oh dear, just as a fly becomes confused by a lit candle,
So do I.
I implore, don't open the window and blow off the candle.
Hold the candle, open the door, and lead me to the garden
of brightness.

Oh dear, just as a baby giraffe does not realize its determination
to stand
So do I.
I implore, don't let me to be preyed upon.
Kick me; show me my determination to stand.

Oh dear, just as a child hesitates to study
So do I.
I implore, don't leave me uneducated.
Punish me; show me that even I can learn.

Oh dear, just as a mountaineer does not see the summit in a
storm
So do I.
I implore, don't leave me directionless.
Throw me the rope; show me that I can climb even in a storm.

Oh dear, just as a calf does not realize fear
So do I.
I implore, don't let me die.
Frighten me; show me that even I can tremble.

These lines he wrote in response to what he thought could be the reason for the perversion in him. He started with some background information but deleted it, for it was too difficult to take and be appreciated as a reason.

Some Background

I am going to talk about a *word*.

The baby, an embodiment of innocence as it may be, compelled by curiosity and means, takes the first few steps toward this *word*.

Even a breast-fed baby would test biting the nipple when it gets its teeth.

As it grows, its environment shows it how best to put this *word* to use. After all, it's the struggle for the attainment of what it feels it needs. (A tormented child may seek to torment another child. Even in innocence, the child may not know that it is doing something wrong.)

As it becomes an adult, this *word* becomes essential for it to perform in the process that leads to procreation. (For some people who may deny it, tell me how to have sex with an undergarment, jeans, and T-shirt on? Even if you do it like that, what would you call it?)

Now having established that this *word* too is part of the qualities which govern human behavior, let's talk about how to handle it.

Why not put this negatively perceived (the way you perceive it and the way you put it to use can be a positive quality) quality to constructive use?

Okay, here we go.

A surgeon does not see nudity but nakedness and medical science.
A general does not see destruction but security and military science.
A priest does not see the devil but God and religious rituals.
A diver may not seek an endangered species but a common pearl.
A driver may not seek adventure but rules of the road.
A sportsperson may not see aggression but sportsmanship.

Okay, enough of my examples. I leave the rest to your creative guessing.

Of course, *education* in the right way at the right time is essential.

At last, this word I acknowledge is *perversion*.

These lines were written to differentiate preference and bias. These lines show that he too is biased and he too has made a justification for his bias. He would like to stress that such bias is not good but is something that one grows accustomed to. He ends up with a hope that this bias does not spoil him.

When Preference Becomes Bias: A Self-Analysis

I have in my life preferred in many instances to eat chocolate.
Do you know what I pick?
The darkest (brownest) and the sweetest.

I have in my life preferred in many instances to eat an apple.
Do you know what I pick?
The reddest and roundest of all in the basket.

I have in my life preferred in many instances to take tea. Do
you know what I have?
The strongest and best aged.

I have in my life preferred in many instances to take fruit juice.
Do you know what I drink?
The mildest and the freshest.

I have in my life preferred in many instances to take rice. Do
you know what I have?
The longest and the leanest.

I have in my life preferred in many instances to take boiled
corn. Do you know what I have?
The toughest (hardest to chew Indian variety) and fattest.

I have in my life preferred in many instances to . . .

I chew, taste, swallow, and my digestive system absorbs the energy and nutrients. So does my preference and bias do a good job?
I hope so.

The one who contains his preference and bias to what he eats, the one who sees variety in preference and bias, the one who relishes the taste, the one who sees unity in a balanced diet, who is he?

These lines he wrote when he had almost lost hope of his love. He had been pursuing love with both his mind and heart, but at this juncture, he put more thrust on his mind so that he could use it to control his heart on the belief that his beloved was married or out of his reach.

Efforts don't go to waste, I thought,
I wanted to draw inferences,
It was more of my mind though,
And less of my heart,
But now an attempt with all my mind and heart,
I wish you are married,
It is not a question of patience,
But a question of wrong inference and dignity,
I take all the wrong on my part,
And give you your dignity,
To do so was I taught,
To do so is my heartfelt intention,
For all the trouble that I have caused,
May I seek forgiveness for them,
Here I am with all the bang,
Waiting for my sweetheart,
No trace of guilt anywhere,
Too quick to say,
But too strong to deny,
For all that is happening is all for my good.

There are always power struggles, and the result of such struggles is human loss and environmental damage. He is just citing a lesson which he learned as a small boy on how such problems could be resolved.

This is a world of alliances. There are only a few messengers who transcend this boundary. If their transcendence serves a purpose, it should serve the purpose of what we call humanity.

I give you a very old example.

In my land, in ancient times there were two kings.
One was powerful and frequently waged war and whose weapons were tarnished by use and soaked in blood.
One was less powerful, was new to war, and whose weapons were oiled and polished and were mere symbols of pride.

Circumstances took them to the events which could lead them to war.

Those days' poets were held in a position of respect by kings.

This is how the Tamil poet Avvaiyar handled the situation of crisis to quell the war.

She visited the court of the less powerful king and used a literary form of false praise to convey her message to him.

She said, 'Oh, great king, your weapons are new and oiled, edges sharp, garlanded, and neatly assembled, but then your opponent's weapons are tarnished by use with bloodstains and blunt edges.' Maybe she said something more and left the king's palace with all due respects.

The war did not happen. This I remember is what my Tamil teacher taught me. You see how such messengers use ingenuity to serve the purpose of humanity?

All praises to them.

This is his attempt to describe God. He understands that such a description will be futile but just gave a try.

That's the power of the Almighty,
There is no shield that the All-Pervading can't pervade,
There is no atom that the Omnipotent can't crack,
There is no element that the All-Creativity can't fuse,
There is no unlovable that the All-Lovable can't love,
There is no demon that can't be humbled by the All-Humble,
There is no illusion greater than the All-Illusion,
There is no clarity than the All-Clarity,
There is no example that can illustrate the All-Example,
No words can describe the All-Indescribable.

(References: the texts of my religion)

This is a letter which he wrote to his manager out of desperation on not doing useful work. His manager just brushed aside his contention and asked him to work on improving the present scenario. One useful thing he deciphered was the place where one can be results-oriented and the place where one can leave it to God.

From
Sathish
Sathish_0077@bingousa.com

To
Mr. David

Sub: I would like to take up a role in the new project.

Sir,

My intentions are that I want to be results-oriented at least in the part where I am governed by the laws of physics.
As far as transcendence to metaphysics is concerned, I can accept anything.
I have no contentions in the statements I have made above.

My approach is that I want to handle both.

I feel that if you permit me to take up a position in the offshore development project there in Technotron Systems, my intentions will be fulfilled.

I feel that I will be able to take up challenging positions eventually in the skills that I am best at.

So please show me a way to purposefulness, for only there will I find contentment and satisfaction.

Thank you.
Yours sincerely,
Sathish

At this point, Sathish was afraid that his thoughts were being read, and so he wanted to escape this situation and wanted to return to India. After this message reached his manager, he was called to meet the manager in his room. His manager asked him, 'Where is the machine?' and he responded by saying, 'I don't know.' Sathish wanted to act like he was innocent and didn't know what had happened to him.

He was actually doing triple action—one within him that is his thoughts, one for the people surrounding him, and one as a machine, which was just a lifeless and emotionless thing wearing the mask of the human body.

For me, all people are equal.

I just want to be of some inspiration.

I am just adamant that my personal preferences are taken care of.

I am not adamant about *caste*, which ails Indian society.

Okay, I'll take up the challenge.

I want to marry a well-educated girl who can take care of me and appreciate my love toward her.

Is my friend Ganesh Swaminathan prepared for it?

I mean, he too will have personal preferences.

But is he willing to forego *caste*?

You must know that in my community, there are a lot of girls that meet the preferences (red, educated, and money) that I have mentioned. I forego all that for a good cause.

Come on, show me a girl.

Be explicit because I am a bit of an idiot, a tube light.

He has many times thought that he had been deprived of a lot of good things in life. But at the juncture before he wrote these lines, he could see how much his country had contributed to its children. This is a song of praise to his motherland.

Fortunate Am I

Fortunate am I for being born in a great country.

What else can a country have given me with all the ills it is struggling to eliminate?

Where else in the world is this much complexity handled with efficiency as is in my country?

Where else in the world is socioeconomic and democratic progress as fast as in my country?

Where else in the world is the human resource which can cope with all this in expert tolerance?

Where else is the natural resource which can support this much population?

Where else is the spirit of resilience as great as in my country when tragedy strikes it?

What else can I expect my country to give me?

It is my turn now, and that is what I am doing.

These lines show his view of what culture could be and is. History is on his side to justify what he means in these lines. He means no offense here, just throwing light on people to respect their tradition and identity.

I feel that a culture that is stagnant is not a culture at all.

A particular society at a particular time and place can change—fact.

Originality is not what I am against.
I want originality to evolve, not convert.
Conversion is a sort of deprivation of originality.

I am not confused between faith and nationalism.

Retain faith in its true place (Pillaiyar Koil), and don't confuse it with nationality.

Nationality is exclusive of faith; it should accommodate Shiva or Jesus or Allah.

This is his own story. He has started from the days of remembrance of his life. There are a lot of lines here that may need explanation. The home that he mentions here is what he disliked as a child, but only later did he realized that his parents were duty-bound and that gratitude had made them reside there. There is always a generation gap; that's culture.

The beginning before birth, I don't know,
The beginning after that, very little I know,
The beginning from the days of remembrance, little I know,
    Silent, I used to be all curiosity within,
    I remember walking through a street of sand that led to the sea,
    To go to school was I told, but I bunked off for fruits of a plant,
    Caught was I.
        Then came I to a new city, a moderate house,
        Good company I found,
        Taken was I to a home which I could not realize then,
        I protested, but no power was I.
A new chapter, a new beginning, and experimentation with curiosity,
Taken to a school was I, fascinated by the playthings there,
I remember children playing and crying and mothers caring for them,
    Prayer, music, and intermittent sleep were my job,
    Playing and fighting were my hobby,
    I ran behind a brother who would give me chocolates,
I remember I beat up my friend, and on summons, I ran,
Caught again was I,
I became the captain of my class, and took I to the stick,
Dropped down was I because of overusing the stick,
    Language, science, and art, I observed and appreciated,
On my home front as well as on my job, rigorous was the pressure on me for what I had to become in the future,
Vacation I used to enjoy, eating and cuddling and visiting,
Then came I to the sixth grade,
So lovely was my miss, and I relished the first beating from her,

My friend pinched me, and I took the matter to my miss,
She rebuked and dismissed me as a silly child,
 To become an artist, I sought at times,
 To become a scientist, I sought at times,
 Of course my experiments with curiosity continued,
The report card, I remember, made me take exile,
Of course caught was I between exile and signature,
I erased the mark on it once and gave myself a pass,
Caught was I,
Days passed very fast and were much the same after each jump
of grade,
I was then inducted as a cadet,
To obey the command in physique and mind was my training,
 I visited a camp, my first venture into the outside world,
 ....
I remember that organ in me took to rigidity,
I didn't know who to ask,
My best knowledge at that time was to keep it a secret,
I continued like that, not knowing what it was meant for,
But then consumed by curiosity was I, wanting to experiment,
Then came a fight and, with it, guilt,
To end my life, I decided,
I knew where I would be rested and wanted to check it out,
 With a turbulent mind on a silent night,
 I walked out to the graveyard,
 Took some pictures,
 What can I say about my cleverness? Very clever.
Then on a chosen day,
I filled the prescription and had on it my father's signature,
I took the tablets, had the blade ready,
I even kept the door open to make it easy for them,

But tragedy, I slept before I could cut my hand,

Then I don't remember; only the pictures showed me,

....
....
....

Knowledge, understanding, I sought again and again and again,

Each mistake took me toward better understanding,

Now I am as I am,

Whatever is learned is a handful of sand, and an entire world is there to be learned.

Sathish wrote the following lines after he woke up in the morning. The night before this morning, he was not able to breathe. He was inhaling and exhaling through his mouth. This he thought was a deliberate act to test his patience. He thought that this was not normal and could be a trick by the authorities. So he decided to stay put.

Sathish's friend Ganesh called him over the phone and asked Sathish to talk to his parents.

Sathish did so and slightly cried while talking to his parents. He said he was not able to breathe properly, and his father, who was a doctor, suggested that he take tablets meant for colds and cough. But even in this situation, he did not reveal anything regarding the machine in his head or the difficulty he was facing. After this call, he bathed in mild-hot water and went back to his room, trying to sleep. He did not go to the apartment of his friend which was nearby as he thought that everyone around was conniving in this plot. He wanted to show off his courage and persistence that he will not succumb to such threats.

After struggling for some hours, he finally slept.

This he wrote when he woke up in the morning
that he thought he would not see at all.

I believe that, with or without it, life should serve its precious purpose.

That morning, he went to a store and selected some cards by assuming that they were from my beloved.

He mentioned the word *assumption*, which by reading others can understand is quite different for him. This assumption made his world brighter and happier and made him appreciate the love of life.

Without you, God,
I don't think
I would have seen this morning.
16 September 2006

Without you, I would have been a machine.
You are still with me.
That's what keeps me alive.
To live, I seek love and money.
But to die, I sought only your love.
16 September 2006

Intuition, dear,
Not assumption.
Only to the outside world is it assumption.
Inside my mind, heart, and soul,
It is love, says my intuition.
16 September 2006

How many anniversaries does God want me to celebrate?
I just want one more anniversary, the last and final one.
16 September 2006

On the following day, he started his writing work as usual.

This was the message he received on his mobile phone to which he intuitively acted upon.

Message: * Silence All *

Action

1. History is history; it can't be rewritten.
2. Let's look for a brighter future.
3. Things take time to change; an aggressive change can cause an unfavorable mutation.
4. You can as an individual pursue change, but you can't make your entire community agree to it.
5. Even within great religions, there are differences, and the proposition 'Let God care for all' should be encouraged.
6. Affection, love, and appreciation of beauty should be encouraged at grass-roots level.
7. There is only trouble in raking up negative issues in history.
8. Each individual should appreciate dignity, self-esteem, and purposefulness, so the individual should be treated that way.
9. There is always room for negotiation; weapons deplete life's purposefulness.
10. World cultures should mingle, and the exchange of culture should encourage humanity, for there are conflicts—not because of God but because of man-made differences.

11. When man makes mistakes, he should be corrected and not tarnished to make him do the wrong or worse.

12. And last, man's basic requirements should be met, which means creativity is also a basic requirement; the others you know already.

*He has a problem of thinking that people laugh
at him when they laugh because of their own reasons.
This is the result of one such laughter.*

I am a joker.
I am happy and make others happy.
I am safe that way.

In these lines, he goes about telling how fear could be accommodated as a component of social well-being.

Fright or Fear

How can we handle fright or fear as a society?

Instill dignity and self-esteem and secular morality (secularity at least in place of education), and make clear to the individual what is of constructive value and what is not.

The individual should be made to appreciate patience and responsibility.

The sense of appreciation of beauty that will result from this will not make the individual a social vandal.

An individual with such a conditioning will not do or fear doing anything detrimental to the values which he has been taught to appreciate.

Of course, we cannot absolutely rule out the stick, but its use should only be secondary and with constructive discretion.

*This is another attempt by him to pacify
any trouble he may have caused.*

* Silence All * Part 2

Speaking scientifically, we all have evolved,
Speaking philosophically, we have evolved too,
We all have a common ultimate origin,
Why do we have so much trouble in accepting a common
ultimate destiny?
'To my heaven, I want to go,' says one,
'No, no, to mine only,' says the other,
We fight for nothing, not knowing that we are all kith and kin,
Our faces may be different, but our purposes should be for all,
Love of all and respect for all and prayers to the All-Ultimate,
It is the white of the sky which splits to a rainbow,
It is in the extensiveness of the dark that the stars shine vibrant
each in their own color,
I don't understand why we persist in differences,
Differences that tarnish and forsake the very reason of
existence,
'I am right,' says one and maims the other,
I ask, is it in maiming that one has to see right?
When we have the road of peace to walk upon,
I don't understand why we persist in the road of danger.

I think I have to explain.

To me, the Bhagavad-Gita, the Holy Bible, and the Quran are
of equal great esteem and respect.

I am talking at the point of social governance and not religion.

I am talking about a scenario where people with all such beliefs merge and mingle.

It is happiness and prosperity that I want, not fighting and misery.

Each religion may have peculiarities, I acknowledge it. That is not what I am against. I want freedom for such peculiarities to persist.

Then where is my contention?

It is the place where all such people mix, like in a classroom, a social gathering, and a government of a country.

Of course, my writings are my personal opinion, and I don't thrust this on anyone. I appreciate the pride of having your own personal opinion.

I am an ordinary person. I may have reacted out of provocation. Just think how another person in my state would have reacted.

Please appreciate that I am a private entity even though I may not have such liberty now.

It is peace that I want; I stress peace that I want.

Please don't draw inferences before you give me time to explain.

I am afraid of live blood, I acknowledge. I say it outside the context of a military scenario (don't misjudge).

My opinions may be ahead of the times and may not be relevant now.
My opinion of reality need not be yours.

These lines are crystal clear in the
message he would like to send.

Dear Indians, How Do We Become a Credible Power?

1. Let's not give in to warmongering.
2. Let's improve our economic status.
3. Let's educate our children.
4. Let's improve our military capability just in case war is thrust on us.
5. Let's improve the divide between village and city (infrastructure, economic zones, schools, etc.)
6. Let's make a good and stable society.
7. Let our old live a respectful retirement.
8. Let's create brands and intellectual assets.
9. Let's make friends with neighbors and other powers.
10. Let's venture and compete in technology (space, nuclear energy, medicine, weapons, whatever)
11. Let's strive for peace and show how good we are in that.
12. Let's create a history of glory.

Then you will see what will happen.

Others seeking greener pastures would want to join us. In being with us, they will see security and stability and prosperity.

These lines he wrote in the starting hours of the office, perplexed on how to start working, confused between love and duty.

Accept it (my love invitation), for how long do you expect me to wait?

Waiting and waiting, I have become tired now,

Caught between my mind and conscience am I,

The mind says, 'Leave it, enough of it,'

My conscience says, 'Don't betray [your love],'

Caught between you and my job am I,

'Do your job,' says my mind,

'First things [love] first,' says my conscience,

Caught between place and duty am I,

'It's the office,' says my dutifulness,

'No, there is no duty greater than the duty of love,' says my conscience,

Caught between reality and dreams am I,

Reality says, 'There is very little chance,'

My dream says, 'Your dreams will come true,'

Caught between vision and discretion am I,

My vision shows me on your side,

My discretion shows me that it's a very feeble possibility,

Caught between firmness and indetermination am I,

'Stay firm, focus on the task at hand,' says my presence of mind,

'Stay there where you can have the fortune of love,' says my conscience,

Confused between conscience and heart am I,

Conscience says, 'It's the mind and heart am I,'

Heart says, 'Only the heart am I.'

I think some people underestimated my understanding,
I understand that only a small perverted section of fundamentalists or fanatics or zealots or inhuman creatures are spoiling the goodness of an entire lot of good people.

I can't demand peace and harmony; at least I can strive for them.
The world needs to get rid of such creatures.

My exaggeration was only an attempt to make my opponents understand.

Before drawing inferences, please give me a hearing. I have a lot more if you can't understand still.

Points:

1. Bamiyan Buddha
2. Constraints or partiality on building new places of worship
3. Human rights partiality
4. Democracy
5. Freedom of speech.

Reserved points:
1, 2, 3, 4, 5, 6, 7, 8, 9 . . .

These lines are meant for people who don't find resources for a high level of spiritual training. These techniques mentioned here are easy and convenient to practice.

Meditation for Idiots

A lot of techniques of meditation are already available; this is my version of the practice of meditation.

Meditation is the psychological and physiological process of bringing the mind and body to a state of harmony.

The turbulence or boredom that is generated in our day-to-day life may make us sometimes feel dejected.

The dejection makes us lose our focus and concentration. The mind may issue orders, but the body may not cooperate. The body may receive impulses, but the mind may not take it. There could also be situations where there is disarray or lack of discipline in the mind–body relationship. Meditation helps us to overcome these issues.

We are an entity where we are mostly controlled by things that are involuntary and where only half or less than that is possible by voluntary decisions or actions.

The meditation process may be initiated as a voluntary process, and the magic, I tell you this, becomes an involuntary habit through practice.

My techniques of meditation are for all; there are no time or money or place constraints.

Okay, let me give you some meditation techniques.

After a good sleep, wake up a bit earlier than when you shoot up to start your day. Keep rolling in the bed for some time, enjoy the comfort of your bed, and allow thoughts to flow, and then sit down, then stand up. Get set and go. Your day has started.

Exercise, a simple exercise, like walking in a park or on a road with greenery or any other place where you can enjoy nature's beauty, will be very helpful.

Enjoy your bath, massage yourself, enjoy the aroma of your soap, take time, and relax.

A simple out-of-the-monotonous job (like ironing your shirt or cooking a recipe), if done with patience and diligence, will improve concentration and give strength to face other rigors of the day.

Playing with children and reliving your childhood will help your craving for a mother's care to come alive.

Of course, prayer and religious rituals are important.

If you can afford sex, have it, do it slow, and don't forget the foreplay.

Enjoy the company of good friends; have a healthy talk.

Listening to melodious music or dancing is a very good technique.

Daydreaming is also useful; when you get time, have coffee or ice cream and daydream.

Spend time with parents and relatives, and care for them; it will give you satisfaction.

Don't expect too much from yourself, do your job with patience, and don't brainstorm too frequently or exert too much physical pressure on yourself.

This is a short story which he wrote on how he could manage life if he married a girl whose customs were different from that of his. The narration of the story is somewhat straight and without literary complexity to keep the message simple.

Ramu and Sita were from the same town. Both were brought up and educated in different schools, each with a repute of their own.

Ramu's family had the repute of having three generations of successful lawyers. Ramu's father was a thriving lawyer and wanted Ramu to become the one to carry forward the family's legacy. Ramu was to marry a girl with an aptitude to support a successful lawyer.

Sita's father was a doctor, a cardiologist. Her grandfather was a general medical practitioner. Sita's family and relatives wanted to see her as a great doctor. It was a matter of carrying forward the family's legacy here too. They wanted her to marry a successful doctor.

Ramu and Sita met in an ice cream parlor, and since they met frequently there, chemistry worked out. So captivated by Sita's beauty was Ramu. So attracted toward Ramu was Sita on hearing about how smart Ramu was in speech.

They one day shared the same table on their friends' request. Slowly their friendship became love, and so it continued for some time.

Time had come for them to pursue their careers. Ramu could not compromise on becoming a lawyer, and so was Sita; she could not compromise on becoming a doctor.

Time passed by; they maintained their communication through letters.

Ramu and Sita finished their graduation, and Ramu started practicing.
Sita's family started to search for a suitable bridegroom for her.

Ramu and Sita met and decided to break their love story to their family.

This was a crucial phase.

They broke the news, and for some time, things were topsy-turvy.

As individuals, they united in wedlock. Opposition could not bereave their love.

Slowly their parents out of love began to meet Ramu and Sita in private. Slowly they got accustomed to seeing them together.

Ramu had become a successful lawyer, and Sita a successful doctor.

Sita conceived, and Ramu was delighted.

But problems began to show up after the baby was born.

On Ramu's side, the customs were different, and on Sita's side, the customs were different. On the basis of day-to-day life, the customs did not bother them much, but when it came to the issue of how the baby should be named, it was a big issue.

Ramu and his side gave up—gave up to the cause of clarity and goodwill.

Time passed by, and love did its work once again. Sita conceived once again.

This time, it was the turn of Sita and her side to give up—give up to the cause of clarity and goodwill.

Ramu and Sita raised their children. One became a doctor and one a lawyer.

Society looked up to them. They had proved in life and livelihood that their love was inseparable. They did this without compromising their tradition and identity.

He listens to movies' songs, and one of the songs in the Tamil movie Ghajini, 'Suttum Vizhi Chudare', may have helped him when he had the drive to write the few lines of romantic text that follows.

Baby, cute and beautiful,
In my dreams,
Into your eyes,
Deep I gazed,
Jumped I into the space,
There twinkled the stars,
I kept flying,
Into the cosmos,
Deeper and deeper,
I lost my weight.

Baby, cute and beautiful,
In my thoughts,
Kissed you straight,
Asking more,
The nectar of your lips.

Baby, cute and beautiful,
Absorbed was I into,
The warmth of your breath,
In and out, you breathed my life.

Baby, cute and beautiful,
Pulling me,
Into the black hole,
Your embrace,
I could not escape.

Baby, cute and beautiful,
The perfume of your scent,
In all this world,
No garden can bear,

The flower that you are.

Baby, cute and beautiful,
What else can I say?
To say or not to say,
I will wait,
I reserve the lines,
For our days,
The days after marriage.

Now what he wrote was a vent to his expressions on listening to two English songs sung by Shania Twain which he downloaded from the iTunes website.

Baby, tell me
What do I do?
What do I feel without you?
Tell me what I do
What do I think without you?
You tell me what I do
What do I work without you?

Come on, tell me, tell me, baby
Is time precious without you?
I keep wasting my time
I keep wasting my energy
All on nothing without you

You tell me, whom do I kiss?
You tell me, whom do I hug without you?

O baby, come on, tell me
What do I learn?
What do I understand?
Other than your love and beauty

Hey, baby, whom do I fondle?
Hey, baby, whom do I cuddle without you?

Oh my darling, tell me, whom do I
Fight with, whom do I quarrel with without you?

Without you, what can sleep with?
What can I research with without you?

Without you, to whom do I sing, 'Sleep, baby, sleep'?

Without you, how can I eat?

Oh baby, tell me, what do I do?
Without you.

What Are Days?

What are days?
Are they movie shows
That come and go?
Oh ho, what are days?
Clinging to the tip
Of my mama's clothing,
Playing and crying
For things small as a lollipop.
Oh ho, what are days?
Will miss shout at me
If I don't sing the rhyme?
Oh ho, what are days?
Why do numbers keep growing,
Making addition and subtraction so difficult?
Oh ho, what are days?
Well, if the world spins,
Won't we slip?
Well, if the world rotates,
Won't the people below fly away?
Oh ho, what are days?
Well, did Newton ask
Why apples fall?
Or did I ask,
Well, if it is right

To speak the truth?
Why did miss then say
We are glued by something
We cannot see?
Yes, she told the truth,
Knowing a tender child's thoughts.
Oh ho, what are days?
Was Einstein better,
Or was Newton better?
Einstein was chased away,
Not so was Newton.
Then why did miss keep telling
Only good boys will
Succeed in life?
Oh ho, what are days?
Why are babies born
Only after marriage ceremonies?
I asked my uncle.
You know what he told me?
Babies are kept in store
In the stomach.
Are only released in the hospital
If mama and papa feel it is okay.
Oh ho, what are days?
They keep coming, but
For how long?
No one knows.
Better enjoy them.
Make the most of them.
For we may not find days
When we need them.

Hey, these are days,
I tell you.
It is true.
These are the days.

After that, Sathish started doing something amazing and not easy for the common man to do. He bought a digital camera and a voice recorder and started making videos and audiobooks.

This is about a mystic situation which Sathish recorded in his voice recorder.

Mysticism

Well, I've experienced levitation in my dream, yes. I am not bluffing. I am true. It happens in my dreams frequently, if at all I get dreams. I don't get erotic dreams, but I get dreams wherein this thing happens frequently. Some sort of feeling where I don't have weight and I fly. I fly to the corners of the room, trying to escape from the ceiling. Yes, a ghostly sort of image tries to free away from my body, and then it just—what you would call—scrapes the ceiling. Okay, what do I mean by *scraping the ceiling*? It touches the ceiling and bounces like this and that, trying to escape from the ceiling, trying to escape from the room.

I am very positive in telling that it is levitation; it is freedom from weight. It is total weightlessness. If I try to recollect that feeling now, it is impossible for me. I don't know if it will be possible for me if I make a very strong effort. By *strong*, it is not strength; it is not physical strength that I am taking about. It's a sort of thing that could be beyond physical power; it could be something that has to do with imagination.

What is imagination? Is it a physical process, or is this levitation that I have experienced beyond the realm of imagination? Well, does this have something to do with spirituality or something like actions of the soul? Why was I not able to escape beyond the ceiling? From the top, I was able to see my body. I was a ghost sort of thing that tried to escape the ceiling and rounded the ceiling. It made rounds on the ceiling, but then I could see my body down.

It could not escape beyond the ceiling. Why was it so? It was spirituality. It could be that this ghost sort of thing was bound to the body. It could be bound to the physical demarcations that are put down while constructing this building, and that was the reason why it could not escape beyond the ceiling. Okay, it could be, but then, I am saying it could be imagination. Okay, there could be a component of imagination, but it is something beyond imagination because in imagination you can't feel the wave.

You see, I said I didn't feel the weight. I was weightless, but I could feel a force, a wavery sort of force, like when an object moves in one direction and suddenly changes the direction and it can feel what we call as force of changing the direction. I observed that. Okay, just jump to and fro, just hop to and fro, and you will observe a sort of feeling. Okay, like in space, the astronauts feel weightless, but when they push themselves to and fro in a confinement, they would be able to feel a wavery feeling.

This thing that was scraping the ceiling was able to get this feeling, so what is this? Just wanted to record this feeling. This could be useful. If I research on why such things happen and keep repeating it again and again and try to recollect, perhaps it could give me an answer to a very significant question. That is the reason why I am recording this. How did it separate from the body? I did not feel it separating from the body, but then what I recollect is that a ghost, a transparent and glassy image or thing, was just whirling in the ceiling and then looking down at the body and that the glassy, transparent sort of thing that was devoid of weight can feel the force of the change of direction.

But then it doesn't happen in my waking state; it happens in my dreams. It happens quite frequently—that is, if I have dreams, this thing happens to me again and again. Erotic dreams, I don't get. Okay, riding a horse, I don't know what I have with riding a horse. Very rarely, when I visited hill stations, have I had a chance to ride a horse, but this thing is secondary to my dreams of levitation. I have had a lot of dreams in this short span of sleep, and these dreams I have had are quite amazing.

This feeling where I was weightless is there; the remembrance of the feeling is there. And okay, if I try to simulate this thing, this feeing where I am weightless, it could be that I can in real time have a sense of what weightlessness is. Yes, I can achieve weightlessness. If I try to simulate the recollection of the trials of memory left behind by the dream, I will have to train my subconscious mind to remember this by repeating to my conscious mind that it has to record this peculiar sort of dream when I get it.

It could be that I can recollect it in real time, the conscious time, and I can use it to experience levitation when I am awake. But then the body stays where it is; levitation doesn't mean that the body flies. Only the glassy thing was moving around the ceiling, but the body as such was down, so I don't think it is a physical phenomenon. I don't think this is something that can be explained by the laws of physics; it is beyond physics, and it could be something like light travelling over vast distances with some sort of intelligence built into it. The glassy thing that I talked about could be something like light. Light travels light years and light years from the origin. The physical light can travel, abiding by the laws of physics.

But then the glassy thing, the thing that has the capacity to experience the force of the change of motion, had a glassy shape of my body. Just think of my body being made of glass with a long tail. Now why did it have a tail? It could be that I could have watched a lot of ghost movies, and I could have imagined the glassy thing like that. This is mysticism and mystic talk.

Your talk looks strange. You don't believe in spirits. You yourself have said that you have not seen God nor the devil, but then this is spiritual, something to do with spirits, something beyond the laws of physics, something with transphysical capacity having intelligence.

My Word

Hey, girl, I give you my word that your chastity is protected in my thoughts.
I know how to discriminate and distinguish; I know what to choose to satisfy my carnal desires. I never indulge with you

beyond the limits of decency. You must know I don't plunder beauty. I don't desecrate the dignity of beauty.

How Do I Look?

Hey, girl, how do I look? How do I look? Do I look smart? Okay, it's all part and parcel or a little amount of your grace, I would say. Now I am a person who is always obsessed about myself, okay? But then a thought came to my mind. Let go what your smile meant to me. But what could your smile have meant to you? Why did you smile at me?

Okay, the answer perhaps to this question could be that you intentionally—mostly intentionally—wanted to do something good to me. After all, why would a girl laugh at a guy who is not that much good in appearance or who is not, let go the appearance even in conduct, the way he talks, the way he behaves, and his smartness?

Putting it all together, why would a girl talk to a person like that? If not talk, at least laugh. Laughter, it's something which is of greater significance. Let go of the talking. Okay, talking too is not of much complexity, but laughter, what made you laugh at me?

I'm thinking on this subject or thinking on why you would laugh at me. It's quite a big subject, don't you see? I'd like to treat it like a subject, your laughter, because if not for your effort of laughing at me, I would not have compiled so many lines of text that could be useful to my book in the future. Hum, hum, you understand? So you have done something significant for me, something very nice, something very great to my life, okay? The drive that I derived from you makes me live this life to the fullest extent.

I derive as much joy as possible from this life, and it is because of you, your thoughts. The more I think about you, the more I enjoy life and the more life means to me, okay? So what is the conclusion?

I've been talking not of things that are of much comprehensible intelligence or intellectuality; I am just giving a vent to my feelings, a vent to my thoughts. You see, my thoughts require some sort of reciprocation, okay? And from whom do I get the reciprocation? From you, the camera, okay?

So what is the conclusion? The conclusion is that you deliberately, intentionally wanted to do something good to me; otherwise, no girl would laugh at a boy like that, okay? I am not a dumb guy. I am intelligent. One other thing I would like to stress is that just because someone has helped you, it doesn't mean that they have become your possession. You can't think about having them as your possession. That is very cunning. You see, that is how a very—what you would call—childish person behaves.

I am not a childish person. I am quite mature, okay? Of course, I may behave like a child. Behaving like a child and behaving childish are different, okay? So let me be a child, a good child, and let me be a mature person—both a child and a mature person, a combination of both. This combination helps me take your laughter in the right sense, okay? What is the right sense? What do I mean by *the right sense*?

Right sense is pursuing my life for my own goodness and for the goodness of people around me, okay? Pursue life not only for your good but for the good of the people around you. For the good of the people who have made you capable of what you are today, okay? For the people who would tomorrow derive some sort of guidance from you, a direction from you, okay? Okay, you see, your face is before me, and your laughter is very near to my eyes.

So when I am talking, I can see your face as I saw it two years ago. So I don't feel like turning off the camera. I want to continue talking. I want to see my face in the screen. I want to see my emotions, okay? But there is no one to reciprocate my emotions, so at last, at last, I switch off the camera.

About Excitement

Hi. Hello. I was just feeling like talking about excitement. And why would I choose to talk about excitement today at this juncture? Today in my office, there was a new consultant joining the duty, and she happened to be a girl. Being a guy, I was excited about having a glimpse of her appearance. Now let me talk about myself for a moment. I am a guy of 29 years, and a guy of 29 years should have proximity to a girl or girls of his age or a woman. At age 29, he should have all this. But then this is something I don't have.

Look at what I have been denied—a very natural thing. A thing that is very basic in life has been denied me all these years. I am not talking about proximity to my mother or my sister. I am talking about proximity to someone of the opposite sex. I should have had sex by now. You look at history, go back 2,000 years, 3,000 years; people would have had all these things, proximity—not only proximity, going beyond proximity. Having sex—they would have had it all by this time. And so they would have had no excitement at my age. But at this age, 29, I am excited at having a look at someone of the opposite sex who has joined my office.

How weird. How crazy. How funny. This is manipulation. What purpose does this manipulation serve? And who have manipulated this? Who are the people who are responsible for this manipulation? Does this serve the purpose of good? Well, I tell you, sex is a birthright, and every man and woman will have to have it at the right time; it is a very natural and basic thing. Now, why does sex always have to be a hidden agenda? Why can't it be straightforward? Why can't it be frank? Why can't it be honest? Why should we always deal with things like sex? Leave sex if you don't want to consider it.

Is love obscene? Is love vulgar? I ask you, why should it be pursued as a hidden agenda? Man, woman, I ask you, why should love be sought as a hidden agenda? Now why do you always require a license for pursuing love? To drive on the road, you require a license. To pursue a career, you require a certificate which your university gives. To become a president of a country, you require the mandate of its citizens.

But then love, whose mandate do you need for love? Why should it be something which has to be pursued, like theft? Why should love be theft? This is crazy, weird, and ridiculous. I know where I come from. I have gone to temples, and I have seen explicit sexual content in the places of worship. The sculptures depict explicit sexual content. Why do you associate vulgarity and obscenity when it comes to love and sex? Would you have been born?

If not for this love and the act of sex, you would not have been born. Why do you associate irresponsibility when it comes to the subject matter of love and sex. If you consider something as a lapse? It is not love. It is not the feeling of sex that is a lapse. It is inculcation that is a lapse. You have been inculcating rubbish stupidity, indecency, and obscenity.

I tell you, a person of my age should not be so excited in meeting a new girl. Now if I feel excited at this age over a person of the opposite sex joining the office. Is it not obscenity or vulgarity that is responsible for this? I don't want to play the blame game. I want justice, humanity. I am asking for a very basic privilege, the right to love and have sex at the right age. I am not being an animal. I am talking of something beyond that. It does not mean that if you have love and you are in love, you have babies. I tell you, we have come beyond those ages.

Everything we do in this world is manipulation. We have manipulated nature, but then this manipulation has been there even before the time of nature that we have observed. There was no life on this planet. How did life come? What was there before this life? There has had been a manipulation—manipulation of nature—and that was why life came into existence. And it is the same sort of manipulation that is happening now. That is the reason why we don't have babies just because we do something like having sex. Evolve, develop, come up, grow up, become mature—I can give you examples, but then if I give you examples, it will become provocative. It may provoke the feelings, so I don't want to go beyond.

Love is a fundamental need. The love that I am talking about and that which a child enjoys or knows or understands are not what a person who is an adult is just okay with. He needs a different sort of love. That sort of love becomes essential when one becomes an adult. Then why, why shouldn't he or she get it? Why should he pursue this love as a perverted idea? Why should it always be perverted? Why can't it be a good thing to ask for?

Phone rings. Okay, let me end up. I need to attend to a phone call.

Well, so far my talk has been very emotional. So I thought that I can take a break. I have had a break for one and a half days. And now I am talking in a very balanced state. I have taken necessary actions, so I've become balanced. So this emotional talk has been out of a state of desperation. I've been starved of something, so my words show emotions and a sense of urgency to attain love.

But I tell you, it is not an easy thing to love. Love—it is not spontaneous. At least to me it is not spontaneous. There are a lot of reactions—both physical and intellectual things—that can happen when one comes to the state of love. We've heard of love at first sight in literature and in some instances in history. To me, love at first sight can only mean infatuation. It is a sort of attraction, only that. Now we can progress from a state of infatuation to love. So if it has happened in literature or history, it could be that this attraction or infatuation has turned into love. But then love, it is a sort of thing that is reached only after a lot of processes—physical as well as intellectual processes—are complete.

Now why do we love? We love so that we can stay together, so that we can live our lives together. That is why the sexes love. Now there has to be an estimation of the cohesiveness of the relationship for the relationship to be termed as *love*. The two sexes that are part of this game of love, what they do is they meet whenever they get a chance to meet and estimate whether the opposite person is okay to have as a life partner.

Of course, attraction is always there, and this attraction is the stepping stone to the next step that leads closer to the step that is love. So when they get a chance to meet, what they do is they talk and look at each other. It is both physical as well as intellectual. The physical compatibility is also important, and the mental compatibility is also important. But the rules are not rigid; the rules in love are not rigid. You never know, there are no hard and fast rules.

They say love is blind; this is very true. Love can be blind, but the meaning of blindness here is not on the level of understanding that the lovers have. It is the degree of strangeness; it is the degree of love being unique. We've had instances of people who are very different in culture meeting together, marrying, having children, living their life, and being happy in their life. There are instances wherein both of them are not equal in physical attraction. They may not be equal in physical attraction, but then they love. It could be that the guy is intellectually good, which she desires, and it could be she is physically attractive, which he desires.

So ultimately, the thing is, you just don't go and propose to a girl by just having a look at her. You calibrate. You estimate. You try to move closer. You try to find signs of compatibility of cohesiveness, and then you move further a step. This is especially particular to people who are quite grown up and who are not so young and naive. A person of 20 years or 21 years may not be so very mature in personality. He may just look at a girl, go straightforward, and propose to her, or she may just go and propose to him. So at that level of maturity, it is okay, but at the level of maturity at the age of 29, there are a lot of complex processes that are involved.

I am not blaming the love at the age of 21 and 22; it happens by attraction, and then it grows. It grows into an understanding and then to a better level of understanding. Then it gets enriched, and then there is a lot of education that is involved. As I have said, if love has some time to progress, it will be very educative. That is why I feel that it has to start early; there has to be an educative curve in love.

And then you can get intimate; you can get physically intimate. There is no rigid rule here too. Physical intimacy, it depends on the culture you belong. If you are from a conservative Indian family, then physical intimacy is a taboo. That may not be so if you are from a modern society. But then one fact is that, in countries where people are more sexually active, there are fewer incidences of sexually transmitted diseases and things like that.

In educative societies where people are active in sex, things like sexually transmitted diseases and sexual violence are very less compared to societies where they say sex is a taboo. It is in these countries that you find that these diseases are more prevalent and that violence and sexually related violence are more prevalent. If sex is a taboo, then the violation of sex too becomes a taboo. It doesn't come up. So the rate is quite higher in these countries where sex is a taboo.

So what was I talking about? I started with a very emotional tone. I was talking out of desperation, and then I took a break so that I could balance myself. And out of the balance, there emerged a better understanding of how to pursue this love. The pursuit has to be in terms of the maturity you are in. Okay, have a great day. Bye.

Evolutionary Judgment

I would like to talk about judgment. What is judgment? I don't know what the dictionary's definition is. But I think judgment is an estimation of what we consider the reality of a situation. Interpretation of what the reality of the present situation is judgment. It could also be an interpretation of the events that had happened in the past. Are we born judges? Judgment is a very important thing in life. It helps us decide what is wrong and right. Judgment is a mixture of discretion, distinguishing, and discrimination. All these things together and the application of these things together is judgment.

When we are born, we come out of the womb and we feel the difference and we cry. Our judgment at the time is very miniscule; it is the discomfort that makes us cry. We judge when we are hungry, and we cry for milk; that is a sort of judgment. It is judging when we are hungry. Then we judge when we want to have the parental attention, and we cry. We judge when to do it and when not to do it. Then we grow up to be a boy or a girl. And then we do mischief.

Is judgment in any way involved mischief? What is mischief? It is a sort of entertainment, and it is an undisciplined entertainment. Mischief is the undisciplined entertainment for small children, which is considered undisciplined by elders. What do we gain out of mischief? We come to know what is right and wrong. The parents say that if you do this, you are right and if you do this, you are wrong. That is what a child's mind takes. At that level, the children take what the parents say as right. If the parents say that it is wrong to talk with strangers, the child will not talk to strangers.

Children do not have the capacity or curiosity then. They could not have understood whether such things exist. Like an enquiry, they may not know what an enquiry is. They may not know that there are situations or words or conditions beyond what their parents say. If the parents say that the police will catch them, they will be afraid of the policeman. If the parents say that the policeman will beat them, they will necessarily be afraid of the policeman. So judgment at that level, at 3 or 4 years, is limited to that extent. Then our needs grow; we begin to start telling lies. Children may not know that they are telling lies when they cry for milk or when they seek the attention of their parents.

When they come up to 6 or 7 years, they come to realize what a lie is. But then still they continue to lie. Can anyone in this world be without telling lies? No, it is impossible; even as a baby, you have lied. How could you have lied as a baby?

Now as a baby, you have needed the warmth of your mother's bosoms or hands. So you have cried just as you have cried for milk. The reason could have been different, but you could have thought that the mother, with the intention of giving milk, would come to you and then hold you in her arms and take you near her bosoms. So you see, even at that level, without knowing of the word *lie*, you have lied. The cries and smile and laughter could have been meant for that. You never know, even a baby could play a lot of tricks without knowing it.

I am not justifying lies but the reason for the lie. If you lie for a good reason, it is not wrong. Children may not have the capacity to judge what is right and what is wrong, so they would just have to take the words of their parents. If you do mischief, the cop will come and beat you. They may not know what a cop is, but they know that beating is painful. They may think that even when it is a caring person like a parent beats them, it is painful, so they could just imagine a stranger beating them. It will be much tougher, so they will come to a judgment that it is painful, and they will be afraid of the cop and will take the words of their parents.

The complexity of our judgment process, it changes as we grow. As a teen, we may not have been at the same level of judgment as when we are 25 or 26 years old. The judgment could be subjective. What is subjective? If you are crazy about something, then you may not hesitate to show bias toward attaining that. So judgment could also be subjective.

As we grow older, we come to know the difference between subjective judgment and objective judgment. Subjective judgment is a weakness, and objective judgment, that's sort of playing tricks or games to attain one's desires. So we should avoid subjective judgment as well as objective judgment. We should concentrate on judgment as such. But then in society, there are a lot of instances where objective judgment and subjective judgment are considered at times rather than real judgment.

Why do we need subjective judgment? A mentally challenged child may not be able to compete with a child who is normal. In a situation where both are made to perform, it is not fair for them to compete. For example, on a simple process like taking food, the challenged person may take a long time, whereas the normal person can take the correct time. But then you don't misjudge; you won't discredit the actions of a challenged child. You just accept it to be equivalent to that of a normal child. So this is subjective judgment; it is subject to the child.

What is objective judgment? Objective judgment is a judgment where we are intent to do something. We have competitions in school, like drawing, running, and swimming competitions. So what is the objective? It is to improve the competition to improve the sportsmanship. So it is reasonable here to use objective judgment.

This might be a good example. There are minorities in a country; they are given special rights in the country, so this is also objective judgment. The bookworm sort of judgment that we follow as a child and teen, it just disappears as we grow older. We are able to judge complex scenarios and situations. But then after becoming an adult, if we tend to judge as a child would, then it is unfair. It is like going to the infancy.

So we will have to evolve as normal people. Our judging capacity should be enhanced. Well, as a child, our mothers tell us that we can take only two chocolates a day. Our mothers might say that if we eat ice cream two times a day, our teeth will decay. But that need not apply to an adult. Even after becoming an adult, if we think of taking only two chocolates or eating ice cream two times a day will be correct then. So what I intend to say is that the rigid rules and laws that we are governed with as a child need not apply to an adult.

Judgment is a learning process. If we are made to judge at a very young age, it will be useful. It will be more productive and useful to the society. Well, take me as an example. As a child, I used to write rules in my mind. I used to have rigid laws as to what is right and what is wrong. But then when I grew up, I changed. I was not able to do justice to the rules and laws that I had framed. I was not able to stick to the rigid laws and rules that I had framed as a child. I was thinking that what my parents and teachers told me was right and that I had to follow it strictly. I did not really put an effort of whether what they said was right or wrong. I just took it blindly that what they said was right because they were bigger and had much more knowledge than me.

You see, these adults, these people who teach children, sometimes compete with children. That is a very funny thing I have observed. How come a grown-up, an adult, competes with a child? The adults here need to use common sense. A child being small is bound to make mistakes. That is what children do; they learn by making mistakes. They have to be given sufficient chances to make mistakes. If given the chance to make mistakes, the right mistakes, they will learn the right way how to avoid such mistakes. They won't commit a wrong or a sin.

Self-Possession

Well, good morning. It is morning now, and I am in a mood to talk as usual. What is going to be the subject of my talk? Can it be the art of maintaining or retaining possessions? Can it be the art of maintaining balance? Call it equilibrium, call it self-possession, or call it maintaining control. So how do I start? I have come to a conclusion of what topic I am going to talk about. It is the art of control. Why do we need to be retaining self-control? What is the purpose behind that? Do we always need to be in control? What is freedom? What is bliss? Are we in control of our freedom, of our bliss? How do we retain control?

We voluntarily think about what is right and what is wrong in our capacity to retain control or possession. Now if we always keep thinking about what is right and what is wrong and then execute it, we will just be like a computer doing calculations, and if we are too much obsessed about being right, then we won't have time for creativity. So making mistakes, giving ourselves a chance to make mistakes, and our desire to make mistakes, even these are control. So I have given a small introduction of what I am going to talk about.

I would like to narrate a small story from mythology. I don't want to be too religious, so I use the word *mythology*. Let me be down to earth. There is a story in Hindu mythology of two holy beasts talking to each other. In Hindu mythology, we have a lot of Godheads, and they have their own vehicles. This is a discussion between the Vasuki, the holy serpent around the neck of Lord Shiva, and Garuda, the vehicle of Lord Vishnu. So from Lord Shiva's neck, the snake asks Garuda, which is a bird of prey, 'Are you doing well?' The bird says, 'If we are where we are and then we talk, everything is okay and good. So we are safe in the place in which we are.'

Why am I telling you this story? This story is very important in the art of retaining possession, the art of control. When we are to enjoy, we need to enjoy to the maximum, and when we need to be sorrowful, we need to be sorrowful or cry to the maximum. What I say may be strange. What is this guy, he says, that he will talk about control and say that when we are to be happy, we need to be uncontrollably happy and that when we are to cry, we need to uncontrollably cry? But then this is very important in the place where we are. I did not mention the place.

When you indulge in sex, see to it that it is safe, but then in the pleasure that you enjoy, experience uncontrollable pleasure. It is very uneventful for me to talk about this, but then I am giving an example. When someone close to you departs, never to come back again, what do you do? You cry, you sorrow— sorrow to the maximum; it is uncontrollable sorrow. What befalls this state of uncontrollable sorrow or uncontrollable happiness is a state of clarity. It is a state where you don't have sorrow or happiness.

So that is the purpose of being uncontrollable in situations where you can be uncontrollable. They call it a state of *shunnya*, or zeroness, in Hindu philosophy. So you reach a state wherein you can start your mind working normally and a state where you can be receptive to day-to-day needs. When do we need control? When do we need to exercise voluntary control? When we are capable of knowing that we are in the wrong way or are about to do something wrong or about to commit a mistake and we can correct ourselves, this is voluntary control. Where could you exercise voluntary control? It could be in your job. It could be in your relationship with your friend. It could be in your relationship with your lover.

So voluntary control is important here. If you indulge in being involuntary or if you can relax your mind's resources in things that deserve uncontrollable attention, like that uncontrollable happiness and uncontrollable sorrow that I have mentioned above, you will have the resources in your mind for calibrated or voluntary control. Now don't be obsessed with what is right and what is wrong in retaining your control, in retaining your self-control.

If someone deliberately insults you, think once or twice whether you really deserve it. If you really deserve the insult, take it. It is your punishment for the wrong that you have done. Feel for it, and mend your ways. Try to correct the mistake that you have made. That is the right way to retain possession or control or equilibrium. If you don't deserve the insult, don't just take it. Don't take it at all. You need not inflict that insult back to the person who is doing it to you. It could be that he is not in control, and so he had done so. Why do you want to compound the problems of a person in distress or who does not know the art of self-retention? Just ignore it and get away from that person. Don't take the insult.

A story comes to my mind; it is a very common story. It is a story about Buddha. Buddha was walking with his disciple on a street. The theme of it conveys the message. Buddha walked with his disciple on a village; it was a narrow road, and it took Buddha through a lot of huts where there were people. The people, on seeing Buddha and finding him strange, abused Buddha verbally, but then Buddha just walked past this shower of abuse, not showing any change in his expression.

Retaining his enlightened state, he walked past. After they walked past the village, his disciple asked Buddha, 'What is this? These people have been insulting you, but then you have just walked past undeterred, and there is no change in you. There should be some sort of anger, an expression of anger in you.' Buddha said, 'I just don't take what they have said.'

So this is the art of retaining self-possession. Know what you must take and know what you must not take. Where did the insults on Buddha go? It went back to the people who directed this insult toward Buddha. Know what you deserve and what you do not. One thing that is very important is that as long as we are in this physical state where our souls reside in your body, we can't hope to be extra physical with persons.

We are people whose souls reside in our body. We are bound to nature, so we need to take care of our bodily needs. This is very important in the art of retaining possession. That is why if pleasure gives you balance, if pleasure helps you in retaining your capacity to judge where you can exercise your righteousness and where you can afford to make mistakes, if pleasure can help you out with this, then indulge in it. Indulge in it in the right amount that will satisfy your desires. I don't want you to indulge in excessive or abusive pleasure.

Pleasure can be experienced in safe and useful ways. It is a pleasure to teach your child something useful in his life. It is a pleasure to plant a tree in your garden. It is a pleasure to watch the sun rise. It is a pleasure to have sex with your beloved wife. That is the sort of pleasure that I am talking about. Aversion to pleasure is not control. Aversion to the reasonable pleasure that we embodied souls are bound to causes us to lose our balance or equilibrium.

We are, as people, capable of knowing when we should be firm on things and when not to be. We should know when we have the liberty of mistakes and when we don't have the liberty of mistakes. What are you going to prove by retaining your firmness? When you say you are firm in doing something, about achieving something, think whether it is really worth the purpose. Be firm. Be persistent. But in being persistent, know your place very well. You could say something that is true. You could say something that is not harmful. But the place in which you are may not be conducive for you to reveal the truth. It is not only true, it is also not harmful, and it is really good, but the place in which you are may not be suitable for you to reveal this thing. So be very aware of it.

What was I talking about? I was talking about self-control and about retaining control. I was also talking about where we can lose our control so that we can relax our minds and bodies. This is a very big topic; it is a very intricate, delicate, and complex art. My efforts in telling this may not be complete even if I make one or more tries. I may not be able to completely and fully express the nuances of this art of self-possession or self-retention.

I may not be in a position to reveal much. I have already talked about judgment. Judge if we are really in need to curtail our actions. Judge whether you can openly enjoy your actions. Judge whether there is really any action in action.

'One who sees action in inaction and inaction in action is a yogi, and he has accomplished all his tasks.' This was something that I read somewhere; it came to my mind. Relax your mind and body whenever you have time for it and in a position for it. When you are at home, when you are intimate with your loving people, your parents, your children, your friends, and your wife, relax. One significant thing that I am going to talk about is, you need not always control yourself. There are instances where you can allow someone else to take control over you.

If you are too tired and don't know what to do, then it is good that you allow some other trustworthy person to take control over you. If you are in distress and if your wife really has experience in quelling your distress, then allow her to take control over you. If she is an expert in judging and delivering what is good for you, then let her take control over you.

After you return tired from the office, where you have tried to cope up with a lot of problems and you have given a lot of solutions, you reach home tired, and you no longer want to be in control, so let her take control over you. Let her care for you. If your child returns from school tired of learning and learning and burdening himself too much with things that he may not understand really, then you take control over him, play with him, tickle him, embrace him. So all these things are important; even being controlled is such a joy. But be careful about who controls you.

Anger—we, in a lot of instances in life, get angry. A lot of events happen, and these events may not be in our favor. We may become angry because of these events which are not in our favor. Anger is different from happiness and sorrow because it is a sort of aggression. How can you control this? You can give a vent to your anger, or you can understand that you are angry and then go about setting things right. When things are set right, you know that you have corrected the problem or issue. You don't have that anger. Don't be angry; don't be angry at all. You may in circumstances act like you're angry because we may have to work with common people. When common people respond to you when you are angry and when they think that they should act only when the boss commands them in anger, you can act as if you are angry.

But I tell you, anger is not good. It is detrimental to the mind as well as the body. So what will you do when you are angry? You first realize that you are angry and then analyze the cause of this anger and try to set it right. Your anger should make you eager to set things right. There should be persistence in your thoughts that you should set things right. And once you have set things right, your purpose is attained, and then anger disappears.

What purpose can anger have? If it has the purpose of insulting someone and then escalating the problem further, then that is not what you should do. But then if it serves the purpose of you becoming eager and energetic in finding a solution to the problem, then it is okay. So that is how you take things in life. That is how you go about dealing with a lot of mood changes. Your mood is not always stable. You sometimes become happy, sometimes you become sad, sometimes you become relaxed, sometimes you become energetic, sometimes you become enthusiastic. Sometimes there is anxiety, sometimes there is hope, sometimes there is desperation, sometimes there is elation, and sometimes there is depression. So there are a lot of moods, and we are bound to these moods.

The art of possession is very important when we are in the state of these moods. If we know that these moods are nothing but manifestations of inadequacies in bodily parameters, we will know how to be independent of such mood swings. If we come to realize that these mood changes are a result of changes in bodily parameters, we will know that we can be stable even in mood swings. We should constantly teach ourselves this art of self-possession or retention.

You may not be happy. You may start the day, but you realize that your son has done something bad. You may become sad, you may become angry at him, and you may have to go to the office. But when you reach the office, you may be in the same state of sadness and anger. But if you realize that the actions that emanate from this state of your mood will be detrimental to the relationships that you may have to manage in the office, then you should mend your actions despite being sad and despite being angry. People will be able to make out that you are sad and angry.

But then if you exercise caution in your actions, they will also say, 'This man, despite being in a state of imbalance, is doing the right actions. He is doing a measured act. He is being very reasonable. He is using his judgment.' Then they will appreciate it. They will tend not to put further imbalance in the state you are in if they are helping. But then if you go to the office and then shout at your boss or shout at your secretary, it will trigger a chain reaction. Then it won't solicit cooperation. It will trigger non-cooperation; people may not cooperate with you. They will think that you are very arbitrary, unreasonable, and irresponsible.

Even in a state of anger, if you are aware of it, you can deliver good action. What else can I talk about self-control? The feelings are very important; there has to be a balance of a lot of feelings. So whenever you get a chance, whenever you feel or come to realize an imbalance or some sort of feeling, try to fulfill it. If you have a strong desire to watch a fiction movie and you haven't been to a movie for a long time, it may not suit your balance. Go and watch it; watch a fiction movie. What's the harm in doing so? Give some time for your feelings too. If you feel that you have been deprived of loneliness for a long time, be lonely. Take a shot. Okay, if you feel that you have to be persistent in being active for a long time or long hours, think whether it is really worth it and whether the situation demands it. If the situation demands it, do it. Don't be a workaholic. If you feel like having alcohol, have it. If you feel like having it but then refrain from being an alcoholic.

Alcohol should help you in retaining control. It should not make you uncontrollable. If you are driving, don't take alcohol. If you are to be fully receptive to stimulus, if you are to be fully receptive to sensory perception or intellectual perception, then don't take alcohol. But then if you want to relax, if you are in safe places where you can lose some amount of your sensory perception and intellectual perception, then take alcohol. It is medicine. The medicine gives you side effects. It is the same thing. It has to be a medicine; it should not become a poison. So I don't advocate alcoholism. It is very bad.

So what else? Okay, as I have told you, one or two attempts at describing the art of retaining possession is not sufficient. I may have to make more attempts. Anyhow, my talk has been very slow. It is because of the nature of what I have been talking about. Okay. Bye. See you.

What Is Life?

What is life? If you ask this to someone who does not believe in God (atheist), the answer would be like what follows:

Life is a manifestation of matter and chemical reactions. Chemical reactions could have triggered atoms to form molecules, both chemical and biochemical. Conditions like lightning, presence of water, sunlight, volcanoes, and oceans could have resulted in the formation of enzymes. Over a long period, microbes could have come into existence. Because of mutation and evolution, plants, insects, animals, apes, and humans could have evolved.

To this person, everything is material in origin. Now let's see what constitutes materials. As an example, let us take an atom of an element. This atom could contain a nucleus, protons, neutrons, muons, etc., and a specified number of electrons revolve around the nucleus in their own specified orbitals. Each element is made up of a distinct number of electrons, protons, neutrons, and other subatomic particles. Each element has its own atomic weight and number. Even energy like light rays and heat is matter.

Is this not intelligence? Besides, processes like nuclear fission and fusion happen in their own discipline. So matter constitutes material, intelligence, and discipline. Matter changes from one form to another—either matter to energy or energy to matter. Matter just remains as matter in all its forms in perpetual time.

Now let us become a theist (one who believes in God) and ask the question 'What is life?' Attach time to matter! We get life, which changes its form with time and also with matter. Our worldly life may be seen as limited by us because of our ignorance of the whole, which is the universe, and God, which is perpetual as time and has no end and beginning. Now after understanding that life constitutes material, intelligence, discipline, and time, let us see what God is. Attach control with life! We get God. You may ask me why. It is because humans think they have control. They may be in control, but they do not have control. Let me explain.

Man does not know what happens to him in the next second or minute. A natural calamity can be predicted by him, but does he know what happens further? A roadside accident can cause him to die. I will tell you why man does not lose his life despite dying. Just note this for a reason. God controls man. Man is in control through God. Even in the peak of his cognizance and conscience, man is just a vagabond moving from one conclusion to another because God moves him—from one birth to another, one minute to another. But why should God be such a sadist? Pain, death, suffering, and besides that, some amount of joy which man experiences?

Well, some men say Allah is the only god. Other men say Jesus is God's only child. Hindus say Shiva is a god and that Vishnu and Brahma are gods also. But at a time in Hindustan 2,000 years ago, Shaivites were saying Shiva is the only *paramatman*. Vaishnavites were saying Vishnu was the only paramatman. The truth is, calling God Allah, Shiva, Durga, Vishnu, Brahma, or Jesus is all the same one's choice and freedom— the freedom of religion and practice of ways of rituals.

Turning Point

Suddenly, one day when Sathish came to his office, an important event took place. His colleagues took away his laptop when he was in the cafeteria. When Sathish came to his cabin, he did not find his laptop, and when he asked his friends nearby, no one gave a reply. He took up the matter to his marketing manager, but he too failed to give a satisfactory reply and did not show Sathish a way to find his laptop. Now Sathish was greatly disturbed and irritated. He felt a sudden nervousness, and his head became hot. Now he understood that this could only be caused by drugs or a machine implanted into his head.

He walked to his rental car parked outside his office and drove straight to his apartment. He walked to his room and lay down, but he could not bear the heat inside his head. He realized that it was a foul act by others. He saw a cockroach in his room and crushed it with a book. He then sought end to his life as well. So he took a pencil knife, and he cut his left hand near the wrist. He completed the thing that was left over from his first suicide attempt. But as soon as he did so, one of his colleagues, Chandrakumar, came by his door and opened it. He tied Sathish's bleeding hand with a cloth.

Sathish was made to sit in a chair in the hall, and some of his other friends arrived. Sathish took a vessel meant for cooking and put his bleeding wrist into it so as not to allow the spoiling of the carpet on the floor. He took a cigar and smoked it, relishing its flavor while he waited to be taken to the hospital. Then two of his friends took him to the car, which was parked by the side of the apartment. On the way to the hospital in Gwinnett County, three black cars followed him.

On arrival at the hospital, Sathish was asked his address, and so he wrote the address of his Indian house near the graveyard. His urine sample was collected, and his bleeding wrist was stitched. He could see a TV in front of him slightly on an elevated platform. The characters in the TV behaved in sync with his thought process. He used to think about George Bush, Putin, and Manmohan Singh, and the characters in TV acted out a sequence to which he responded by thinking. This happened for half an hour and, after deriving political substance from his thoughts, came to an end.

Sathish stayed in the hospital for fifteen days, and while there, he got a pen and some papers and started writing the following.

Parables

There was a monk. On his journey, he had to sleep. He found a place under a tree. After lying down, he looked up. It was a giant tree, but its fruits were small. He thought that it was stingy for the giant tree to bear such tiny fruits. The pumpkin and the tiny creeper came to his mind. Suddenly he woke up after falling asleep. A fruit had hit his cheeks. Now he realized, had it been a pumpkin, he would not have been alive.

Sathish was a good cyclist. He enjoyed cycling. His uncle had a bike, and Sathish's cousin Senthil used to drive it. Sathish used to be jealous then. He demanded that he too be allowed to drive the bike. His uncle helped him. Sathish wanted quick results. So he took the bike when his uncle was not there. He sat on it and gave the bike full throttle and accelerated. He was not able to balance, and in fear, he gave it a full throttle and smashed the bike on a gate a few buildings away. However, people came to his rescue and helped him, and he was safe. His bruises disappeared a few days after.

As a school child, Sathish was taken to a school for the blind. He saw blind people not only happy but doing hard work. They were weaving carpets, and he saw them read using poked cardboard (Braille). He saw them singing and playing music. He was just a child and did not realize the purpose of all that. Now that he is grown up, when events make him think about what he can do, he remembers them. What could be the lesson he learned? There is joy and satisfaction only in work. As long as we work, and we are content we satisfy a purpose. Our life is fruitful.

This is a story of a king and an emperor.

The kingdom was on a hilly terrain. Rivers flowed, and it was rich in flora and fauna. Medicinal herbs to cure almost all diseases were found. The king nurtured the art of medicine. The emperor, who was a close friend of the king, suddenly became ill. His courtiers could not find an immediate cure. So they sent forth messengers to all the kingdoms for a medicine. The king received the messenger. He remembered how the emperor helped him overcome conquerors and famine. He immediately dispatched a medical team. The emperor was then cured. The emperor promised that as long as his empire flourishes, so will the kingdom flourish. People celebrated, and the friendship flourished.

This is a story of a painter and a blacksmith.

The painter is a great artist. Kings were ready to trade gold and gems for his magnificent painting. The artist was a genius; he secretly kept his precious painting in a wooden box, thinking that he could sell this art to wealthier emperors for a greater price. Suddenly there was a great storm; there were floods, and people were fleeing the city. The blacksmith remembered the artist because he had made him a wooden box. He had an iron box which was waterproof, his trade secret. He took it out and gave it to the artist. The artist thanked the blacksmith. The blacksmith thanked the artist. Both of them returned to their kingdom. Their goal now was to make their king proud. The kingdom prospered.

This is a story of a vagabond hunter and a farmer.

The hunter lived in the jungle and hunted animals for food. He used stones and twigs to burn the flesh and eat it. One day while hunting, he chased a deer. Unfortunately, he fell down and broke his leg. He was immobilized. A farmer came to the jungle to collect wood. He rescued the hunter and took him to his hut. In a couple of weeks, his leg was cured. The important thing was that he learned the ways of the farmer and decided to be a watchman or guard to protect him against wild animals. The hunter thought of how miserable his life was in a cave and treetop. Now he had a hut, oil for cooking, and food grains for a good meal.

This is a story of a woodcutter and a scholar.

Both of them were on a journey. The woodcutter saw the scholar at a market. The scholar advised the people assembled on what is right and what is wrong. The people listened to the scholar and praised him for his lessons. On the morning soon after sunrise, both of them started on their journey. The woodcutter joined the scholar after making due requests. The scholar accommodated him. The journey took them through a jungle after they passed the town. Suddenly a tiger approached them and pounced on the scholar. The woodcutter used his axe and drove the tiger away. The scholar thanked the woodcutter for saving his life. The woodcutter thanked the scholar for all the good lessons which he received on the way.

A Buddhist's Story

There was a warrior with pride in his might and courage. He had not seen the divine. One day he heard of a monk. People said he was divine. The warrior became arrogant. He went straight to the monk and ordered the monk to show him the divine. The monk tacitly ridiculed the warrior. The warrior raised the sword.

The monk said, 'You see evil now.'

The warrior put the sword back in its sheath and was humbled before the monk.

The monk said, 'You see divine now.'

Sathish, Hema, and Lavan were children. They played and used to chat. They liked to hear stories. One day Sathish told a story slowly but steadily. Hema and Lavan enjoyed it. The next day Sathish came up with another story and did not know how to finish it.

Lavan said, Your stories are fake.' She proved her point by asking Sathish to show her the book where he read this story.

Sathish thought that his stories were really fake. Only after he grew up did he realize that indeed his stories were his own and were real.

Johnny was an inquisitive person. He wanted to buy a radio. He searched and found the best one that met his criteria. On the second day, the radio stopped playing. He was confident that the transistor had burned out. So he went to an electronics shop and replaced the transistor. Still the radio did not play. He was now confident that the capacitor had burned out. So he replaced it. Still it did not play. Finally, he took the radio to an electrician. The electrician used an ammeter and found the battery defective. Now Johnny's radio became a refurbished radio.

This is a story of a doctor and a patient.

The doctor was an experienced person. The patient came to the doctor and said he had memory problem. The doctor checked the patient and said he is okay, and he sent the patient away.

The patient forgot to take his pen to the office. That evening, he came to the doctor, complaining about memory loss. The doctor gave him some vitamin tablets. After a week, the patient forgot to pay his telephone bill. That evening, he came to the doctor, complaining about memory loss. The doctor had no other go but to suggest an invasive operation. Guess what the patient did. He was happy and nodded. God help the doctor.

Letter to Madhu

Hi. I am Sathish. You could have forgotten me. I was just one among the hundreds that you deal with in your life. Madhu Malar, I wish you all the success in your career. You don't know that you have been a source of inspiration in my life.

I took the liberty and advantage but did not disgrace it. You will continue to be my source of inspiration. I am about to get married. And I would like to thank you for making me worthwhile. My wife will be my life partner. I will show her all respect, love, and responsibility. If I can derive inspiration from a girl whom I met six times, imagine what all that my life partner will contribute to me.

On the thirteenth day in the hospital, Sathish became impatient and wanted to see the outside world. He spoke to his father over the phone and informed him about his desire to come to India, and his father accepted his proposal.

Sathish wrote the following letter to the doctor treating him.

To Doctor Mam:

Mam, I am not a PhD. I don't have a doctorate degree. I am neither a religious scholar. I am one among 100 crore common Indians. That is my background. Please tell me how best a person in my situation should face circumstances. I am not an expert in the art of the bourgeois or high-class elegance or expression.

If I have offended you, the best I can say is 'Please forgive me'. I owe my living to a lot of my well-wishers, friends, and family members. I look forward to working toward our well-being.

On the fifteenth day in the hospital, Sathish's brother-in-law came to the hospital to accompany him all the way to India. Sathish was taken to his office in Suwanee for the last time so that he could sign some papers in the presence of his brother-in-law and his marketing manager. That was at about

7 p.m., and all along the way, the sidewalk was decorated with lights, but there was no light in the buildings on both sides of the road. When he reached the office, he saw that the only building that was illuminated as far as his eyes could see was his office. After waiting there for a few minutes, his marketing manager opened the front door. All of them went to the manager's room and sat in their respective seats.

The manager asked Sathish, 'Did you cut your hand?'

Sathish said, 'Yes,' and showed the bandage on his wrist.

After Sathish signed the papers, his manager said, 'You will do well.'

Sathish then went to his cabin in the office and stared at his workplace, and then they left the office. Sathish returned to India and is now leading a happy married life with two children, leading a low profile life in his hometown. Sathish thinks, 'They say the first impression is the best impression, but I have left a lasting impression.'

Life will continue.

Glossary

1. Pillaiyar: God Ganesh(Hindu God with elephant face)
2. Shaivites: **Followers of Shaivism. Saivam** or **Shaivism** or **Saivism** (<u>Sanskrit</u>: शैव पंथ <u>Tamil</u>: சைவவம், *śaiva paṁtha*; lit. "associated with <u>Shiva or Saivam</u>"), is one of the four most widely followed sects of <u>Hinduism</u>, which reveres the god Shiva as the Supreme Being. Followers of Shaivam, called "Shaivas," and also "Saivas" or "Shaivites," "Saivarkal," believe that Shiva is All and in all, the creator, preserver, destroyer, revealer and concealer of all that is. Shaivism is widespread throughout India, Nepal and Sri Lanka. Areas notable for the practice of Shaivism include parts of Southeast Asia, especially Malaysia, Singapore, and Indonesia.
3. Vaishnavites: **Vaishnavism** (*Vaisnava dharma*) is one of the major branches of <u>Hinduism</u> along with <u>Shaivism</u>, <u>Smartism</u>, and <u>Shaktism</u>. It is focused on the veneration of <u>Vishnu</u>. Vaishnavites, or the followers of the Vishnu, lead a way of life promoting differentiated monotheism (<u>henotheism</u>), which gives importance to Vishnu and his <u>ten incarnations</u>.
4. Vasuki: Vasuki is famous for coiling around the neck of Lord Shiva. Lord Shiva blessed Vasuki and wore him as an ornament. The most famous legend in <u>Hinduism</u> in which Vasuki took part was the incident of <u>Samudra manthan</u>, the churning of the <u>ocean of milk</u>. In this legend, Vasuki

allowed the <u>devas</u> (gods) and the <u>asuras</u> (demons) to bind him to <u>Mount Mandara</u> and use him as their churning rope to extract the ambrosia of immortality from the ocean of milk.

5. Garuda: The **Garuda** (<u>Sanskrit</u>: गरुड *garuḍa*) is a large <u>mythical</u> <u>bird</u>, bird-like creature, or <u>humanoid bird</u> that appears in both <u>Hindu</u> and <u>Buddhist</u> mythology. In <u>Hindu</u> religion, Garuda is a <u>Hindu</u> <u>divinity</u>, usually the <u>mount</u> (*vahana*) of the Lord <u>Vishnu</u>. Garuda is depicted as having the golden body of a strong man with a white face, red wings, and an eagle's beak and with a <u>crown</u> on his head. This ancient deity was said to be massive, large enough to block out the <u>sun</u>.

6. Koil: **Koil** or **Kovil**, "King's House" is the Tamil term for a distinct style of Hindu temple with Dravidian architecture.

Oh dear, just as a fly becomes confused by a lit candle,
So do I.
I implore, don't open the window and blow off the candle.
Hold the candle, open the door, and lead me to the garden of brightness.

Oh dear, just as a baby giraffe does not realize its determination to stand
So do I.
I implore, don't let me to be preyed upon.
Kick me; show me my determination to stand.

Oh dear, just as a child hesitates to study
So do I.
I implore, don't leave me uneducated.
Punish me; show me that even I can learn.

Oh dear, just as a mountaineer does not see the summit in a storm

So do I.
I implore, don't leave me directionless.
Throw me the rope; show me that I can climb even in a storm.

Oh dear, just as a calf does not realize fear
So do I.
I implore, don't let me die.
Frighten me; show me that even I can tremble.

This book is about life, inspiration, meditation, sexuality, and above all, love. This is a real life story and a source of inspiration to many. The hero of the story is leading a successful, satisfied and content life despite having had faced tough times in his youth. The author also sometimes becomes poetic. Most of the contents are inspired from the author's own experiences.